She
Persisted

....

FLORENCE
GRIFFITH JOYNER

....

—INSPIRED BY—

She Persisted

by Chelsea Clinton & Alexandra Boiger

· ·

FLORENCE GRIFFITH JOYNER

· ·

Written by
Rita Williams-Garcia

Interior illustrations by
Gillian Flint

PHILOMEL

PHILOMEL BOOKS
An imprint of Penguin Random House LLC, New York

First published in the United States of America by Philomel Books,
an imprint of Penguin Random House LLC, 2021.

LIBRARY OF CONGRESS CATALOGING-IN-PUBLICATION DATA
Names: Williams-Garcia, Rita, author. | Flint, Gillian, illustrator. Title: She persisted:
Florence Griffith Joyner / written by Rita Williams-Garcia ; interior illustrations
by Gillian Flint,. Description: New York : Philomel Books, 2021. | Series: She
persisted | "[I]nspired by She Persisted by Chelsea Clinton and Alexandra Boiger." |
Includes bibliographical references. | Audience: Ages 6–9 | Audience: Grades 2–3 |
Summary: "A chapter book biography of Florence Griffith Joyner, part of the She
Persisted series"—Provided by publisher. Identifiers: LCCN 2021009713 |
ISBN 9780593115954 (hardcover) | ISBN 9780593115961 (trade paperback) |
ISBN 9780593115978 (epub) Subjects: LCSH: Griffith Joyner, Florence Delorez,
1960—Juvenile literature. | Runners (Sports)—United States—Biography—
Juvenile literature. | African American women—Biography—Juvenile literature.
Classification: LCC GV1061.15.G75 W55 2021 | DDC 796.42092 [B]—dc23
LC record available at https://lccn.loc.gov/2021009713

Printed in the United States of America

10 9 8 7 6 5 4 3 2 1

Edited by Jill Santopolo
Design by Ellice M. Lee
Text set in LTC Kennerley

To
my daughters,
MRG, *hurdler, and* SEG, *shot-putter*

She Persisted

DEAR READER,

As Sally Ride and Marian Wright Edelman both powerfully said, "You can't be what you can't see." When Sally Ride said that, she meant that it was hard to dream of being an astronaut, like she was, or a doctor or an athlete or anything at all if you didn't see someone like you who already had lived that dream. She especially was talking about seeing women in jobs that historically were held by men.

I wrote the first *She Persisted* and the books that came after it because I wanted young girls—and children of all genders—to see women who worked hard to live their dreams. And I wanted all of us to see examples of persistence in the face of different challenges to help inspire us in our own lives.

I'm so thrilled now to partner with a sisterhood of writers to bring longer, more in-depth versions of these stories of women's persistence and achievement to readers. I hope you enjoy these chapter books as much as I do and find them inspiring and empowering.

And remember: If anyone ever tells you no, if anyone ever says your voice isn't important or your dreams are too big, remember these women. They persisted and so should you.

Warmly,

Chelsea Clinton

FLORENCE GRIFFITH JOYNER

TABLE OF CONTENTS

....

·····························

A Girl Called Dee Dee

Florence Griffith Joyner was an Olympic champion who won gold medals and broke world records as a sprinter. But before there was Florence Griffith Joyner, or "Flo-Jo," there was a girl called Dee Dee.

Long before she was born, her newly married parents, Robert and Florence Delores Griffith, lived in a small town in the Mojave Desert, where their family grew. The Mojave Desert spans from southeastern Los Angeles, California, to parts of Nevada, Arizona and Utah, and the Griffith family lived in the area near Los Angeles. The Mojave Desert is a hot, dry, wide-open space with mountain ranges, sagebrush and red desert blooms on tops of prickly cactus plants. The calls of owls, coyotes and bobcats peppered the night air. In the daytime the Griffiths' backyard was plentiful with lizards, snakes, slow-moving tortoises, fast jackrabbits—and kids!

In 1959, Christmas came early for the six Griffith children. On December 21st, Bobby, Weldon, Vivian, Kathleen, Robert and Elizabeth welcomed their seventh sibling, Delorez Florence Griffith, into the family.

Delorez Florence Griffith was named after her mother, Florence Delores. Mrs. Griffith wanted her daughter to be her own unique self. So, her first name, Delorez, had its own spelling, and Florence was her middle name. The Griffiths took to calling their newest family member Dee Dee.

Mrs. Griffith saw something special in each of her seven children. In Dee Dee she saw a child who seemed to float like a ballerina as she moved. But Dee Dee was also speedy and earned another nickname, Lightning, as she ran through the house.

Mr. and Mrs. Griffith found ways to keep their children's minds and bodies active. Mrs. Griffith, a fast runner, played racing games with

her children. She would line them up and call, "Ready, set, go!" Off they'd run! Even though Dee Dee's brothers and sisters were older, that didn't stop Dee Dee from racing to win.

By the time Dee Dee was four, she had six brothers and four sisters—many who already attended school. Dee Dee looked forward to starting school with her siblings, but her mother had other plans for her children's education. Much to Mrs. Griffith's disappointment, her children could only attend segregated schools for Black children. Her husband, an electrical technician, worked hard. But like his African American co-workers, Mr. Griffith struggled to earn a fair wage. These unfair practices only reminded Mrs. Griffith of the racial discrimination and segregation that she had grown up with in the South and hateful practices that were clearly present beyond the South, too.

Mrs. Griffith had had enough! She was tired of waiting for things to improve for her family and made a big decision. It was also a hard decision. She decided to leave the segregated desert town and separate from Mr. Griffith. Dee Dee loved her father so. It pained her to be apart from him. But her mother remained firm in her decision. Dee Dee, along with her ten siblings and mother, moved to Watts, California.

Watts was a low-income neighborhood in Los Angeles with few employment opportunities. In 1965, growing conflicts between the people of Watts, mainly African Americans, and the police, resulted in one of the largest riots of those times. On August 11, White police officers attempted to arrest a Black motorist who was suspected of drunk driving. A scuffle ensued between the man and the police. To the people in the neighborhood who had gathered and witnessed, the scuffle had turned quickly into police brutality, where the police use more force than they need to get someone to do what they tell them to do. The people of Watts felt they had lived with police brutality long enough. The uprising that resulted lasted for six days and was called the Watts Rebellion.

The Watts Rebellion had not yet happened when Dee Dee and her family moved to the Jordan Downs Projects—public housing made affordable for low-income families. Mrs. Griffith knew of the problems that surrounded their neighborhood. She saw Jordan Downs as a first step on their way to better opportunities and told her children, "Start walking."

Dee Dee was too busy keeping up with her siblings to know that they had moved to a low-income neighborhood. She saw pink townhouses with palm trees along the sidewalks. She darted between laundry that hung on clotheslines in the backyard. She played football with her brothers, and they played rough! Her older brothers wouldn't let her join in if she cried. So, Dee Dee ran lightning-fast with the football, and if she was tackled, she didn't cry.

In the evenings, Dee Dee gathered among her family to share thoughts—good, bad or ordinary. Each week the Griffith children took turns reading from the Bible. At five, Dee Dee could read well and held her own in family discussions.

Mrs. Griffith kept her children busy, but keeping busy didn't fill the longing in Dee Dee's heart. She missed her father greatly. She wasn't alone. Her mother understood her children's feelings. During the holidays, Dee Dee and her siblings visited him in the Mojave Desert. The Griffith brood were free to run about in wide-open spaces. Watching Dee Dee run through the house gave Mr. Griffith an idea. He challenged Dee Dee to race the jackrabbits that ran around in their backyard.

A jackrabbit is actually a hare, and not a rabbit. Unlike its fluffy cousin, a hare has shorter fur and a longer, leaner body. Its long pink ears are almost see-through and stand straight up on its head.

Dee Dee was up for her dad's challenge. She studied the movement of jackrabbits. The way their long legs stretched out as they bounded through the air with grace. She saw how jackrabbits didn't hop. Jackrabbits raced!

During the Christmas break, Dee Dee raced jackrabbits across dirt and sagebrush in the hot, dry desert. She got faster and faster. Then one day she caught a jackrabbit. That jackrabbit had escaped coyotes, bobcats and owls, but it couldn't outrun Dee Dee.

CHAPTER 2

Everything!

Dee Dee was both worried and excited to start school. Shy and quiet, Dee Dee was more at home among her siblings. Still, she was excited to learn. And when she left the house, her mother told Dee Dee she was free to style and dress herself in her own unique way. She went to kindergarten in different-colored socks and wore a long braid that stood straight up on her head— almost like a jackrabbit's ear!

When her classmates laughed at her, Dee Dee didn't seem bothered on the outside, and laughed along with them. But on the inside she was hurt and held back her tears until she was in the safety of her home. Her mother consoled her and told her to "*just move on.*" Dee Dee found comfort in her mother's words and kept them close to her heart.

Her teacher asked Dee Dee, what did she want to be? Without hesitating, Dee Dee said, "Everything. I want to be everything." Her classmates laughed, but this time, Dee Dee didn't laugh along, and she didn't cry about it later. Dee Dee meant what she said: she wanted to be everything.

At age seven, Dee Dee joined the Ray Robinson Youth Foundation. Former boxing champion "Sugar" Ray Robinson started the foundation to "give back" to neighborhood children like Dee Dee, whose families didn't earn enough money for everyday needs. It wasn't long before the speedy seven-year-old won first-place ribbons in running.

Dee Dee was shy, but she wasn't afraid to race. After all, she could outrun jackrabbits!

There was nothing one-sided about Dee Dee. She taught herself to balance on and ride a unicycle. She had a huge pet snake that she wore confidently around her neck. Her father always challenged her to do hard things, so to face her shyness, she starred in a school play. But Dee Dee also loved to sew clothes for herself and her dolls, write, draw, paint and create her own nail polish and hair ornaments. Most of all, like her mother, Dee Dee loved fashion! She spent many afternoons trying on her mother's dresses and always found ways to stand out in her colorfully self-styled track outfits. Dee Dee's talents and interests were endless!

At fourteen, Dee Dee won first prize at the Jesse Owens Arco Games, a race sponsored by

Olympic gold medal legend Jesse Owens. Dee Dee didn't know who Jesse Owens was. She only

wanted to race and travel! Dee Dee treasured her prize, a trip to San Francisco. Seeing different sights only made her want to travel more. The following year, Dee Dee entered the Arco Games again hoping to win the first-place prize, a trip to Texas. Dee Dee won first place and couldn't wait to plan her trip. But the bad news came to her from Jesse Owens himself. She had already won last year. The trip to Texas would go to the second-place finisher. Dee Dee was devastated and couldn't fight back the tears streaming down her cheeks. She had won! It was unfair! Eventually, she remembered her mother's words: "Move on." And she did.

By high school, Dee Dee wanted to be known by her middle name, Florence. Her siblings still called her Dee Dee, but at Jordan High School, she was Florence Griffith. There, Florence joined the track and field team as a sprinter and a long jumper. For the first time, she wore a team uniform instead of her own creations. Still, she persisted and found a way to show her individual style: leggings under her track shorts! It wasn't long before her teammates followed Florence's style and also wore leggings with their uniforms.

Florence found running 400-meter relay races with three teammates different from racing as an individual. In relay races, each girl runs one part or one "leg" of the race. The fourth or "anchor" leg is run by the fastest sprinter on the relay team to make up any time lost by the other runners. Florence quickly adjusted to her role as Jordan High's fast anchor.

As a high school senior, Florence prayed, trained hard and wrote her goals in her diary. One of her goals was to attend college in the fall and join the track team. She wasn't alone in her athletic and academic goals.

Valerie Brisco, another fast sprinter, also lived in Watts and attended a rival high school. Valerie had her own inspiration. She dedicated her races to her older brother, Robert, a track star who had been killed by a stray bullet while he worked out. Valerie might have noticed the fast Griffith girl, but if she did, she didn't show it. Valerie would line up in the starting blocks, take off and beat Florence in every race.

For the first time, Florence had real competition on the track—someone else faster than a jackrabbit. But Florence didn't worry. Competition only drove her to train harder and run faster.

. . . .

CHAPTER 3

Inches Away

Florence earned excellent grades in high school, and broke records in sprinting and in the long jump. Still, she did not receive a college scholarship. Money was tight in the Griffith home, so Florence worked odd jobs to pay for school. She was able to raise just enough money for her first year of college at California State University at Northridge in 1978.

Florence immediately joined the track team.

She was happy to be on the team, but she wasn't happy to wear the team's uniform. The women's uniform was the same as the men's uniform. The shorts and tank tops were boxy and masculine. When Florence saw herself in the team uniform, she didn't see her own unique style or love of bright colors. She didn't see Florence.

However, when her coach, Bob Kersee, saw Florence, he saw her talent and determination. He showed Florence techniques to improve her form and her ability to run fast but relaxed. Florence wanted to improve, although running relaxed didn't quite make sense to her. Still, she followed Kersee's coaching. Hard work and learning new methods paid off. In her first year at Northridge, Florence helped her team win the National Collegiate Athletic Association Championship title.

While many athletes struggled in class, Florence earned As. She should have been on top of the world, but she worried about not having enough money. Her classmates drove cars while Florence rode buses for long distances to get to class. She didn't always have enough to eat, and most of all, she struggled to pay for her education. So Florence made a big decision. A hard decision. At the end of her first year of college, Florence left school. She took a job as a bank teller to save money and to help her mother. Florence dropped out of school, but she was determined to return.

Coach Kersee understood Florence's struggle to pay for college, but he didn't want to lose his talented sprinter. He helped Florence find money for college through grants, loans and scholarships. But that wasn't enough for Coach Kersee. He sat with her and guided her as she filled out the many financial aid forms. After a year away, Florence was back in school at Northridge, this time with her former rival, Valerie Brisco.

In the meantime, Coach Kersee was becoming a star coach. Other schools wanted him to work with their athletes. He left Northridge and went to UCLA, a school with a bigger track and field program.

Florence didn't stay at Northridge for long after he was gone. By 1980, Florence transferred to UCLA to train with Coach Kersee. She worked hard to stand out among the other talented sprinters, and once again, her hard work paid off. She was invited to try out for the 1980 Olympics. Florence's hopes soared with possibilities. Imagine winning an Olympic gold medal! Coach Kersee had faith in her. More important, Florence believed in herself. She put in long hours to train in hopes of winning one of three spots on the Olympic team.

That summer Florence packed her bags and traveled to Eugene, Oregon, for the 1980 Olympic tryouts, or "trials." She relished the chance to see more of the world beyond Los Angeles. But she also looked forward to racing in clothing that made her feel good and look good when she ran, since there were no uniforms at the Olympic trials.

In Eugene, she met a handsome triple jumper named Alfrederick Alphonzo Joyner, a student from Arkansas State University. He was the brother of Florence's UCLA teammate and friend Jackie Joyner. It was clear that Al liked Florence, but Florence was focused on her goal to get one of the three spots needed to make the 1980 Olympic team.

Florence lined up to run the 200-meter race. She pushed herself hard off the starting blocks. As hard as she pushed off and

then pumped her arms, she came in fourth place. Florence lost her chance to make the 1980 Olympic team by mere inches.

One of the athletes to make the Olympic team was her former Northridge teammate Valerie Brisco.

Florence was deeply disappointed with herself. She made a promise: she would make the 1984 Olympic team. Her promise wasn't an empty promise. While the Olympic teams traveled to Europe and to the White House, Florence persisted in her pursuit of her Olympic goals. She spent her summer at the track every day, and pushed herself to improve, just like she had so many years before when she was determined to race and beat the jackrabbits in the Mojave Desert.

The National Collegiate Athletic Association,

or NCAA, is an organization that maintains rules and policies for college sports throughout the country. They are most known for supporting and awarding college sports competitions, or championships. To win an NCAA championship is often the top achievement of a student's athletic career. In her junior year Florence ran the 200-meter race and won her first individual NCAA title. It wasn't a team title, but her title alone.

Within her chest thumped the heartbeat of a true champion. But to be an Olympic champion, she must make the team. To make the next Olympic team, she would have to train even harder.

CHAPTER 4

· ·

Bittersweet

Florence's graduation from UCLA in 1983 brought great joy to the entire Griffith family. That June, Florence's nieces and nephews beamed with pride for their aunt. Florence was their favorite babysitter, tutor and storyteller. Now she had earned a college degree in psychology. Their aunt was unstoppable.

Florence immediately set her sights on competing in the Olympics and winning a gold medal.

But first she had to make the 1984 Olympic team!
Over the next year, Florence worked long hours
with Coach Kersee to be in top form. With the
trials in Los Angeles, Florence had the advantage

of competing before cheering hometown fans. And, once again, she didn't have to wear a team uniform. She was free to be Florence!

The other runners at the Olympic trials wore shorts and tank tops. Florence wore a bright shining green unitard with leggings. Sports reporters dubbed her "Fluorescent Flo" because of her bright shimmering outfits. That wasn't all! Fluorescent Flo's fingernails were more than four inches long—and were painted bright red. Expressing herself through her own unique style gave Florence confidence. *"Dress good to look good. Look good to feel good. And feel good to run fast!"*

Florence needed that confidence to run the 200-meter trials in lane seven. Runners in lanes seven and eight—the outer lanes—can't see the other runners around them. Florence wouldn't know if she was ahead or behind the other runners until after she made the turn. That might be too late!

Still, she remained calm. Even in the outer lane, Florence felt she could win. She crouched down into her position, ready to run the 200-meter race. She heard the starter's pistol, pushed off the starting blocks and ran as hard as she could. How could she run relaxed when this race meant everything? Florence finished second and made the Olympic team! The first part of her dream had come true! She hugged her former college teammate Valerie Brisco-Hooks, who was now married, a mother and the first-place finisher.

Two months later, the 1984 Summer Olympics were also held in Los Angeles. Florence was ready to show off her explosive speed in the 4x100 relay.

But it wasn't Florence's speed that created excitement. Many wondered if she could pass a baton in a relay with such long fingernails. Defiant Florence wouldn't let their doubt bother her. "That gave me fuel to try even harder."

Florence hoped to win a spot on the 4x100 relay, but the US team officials, who select the sprinters for the relay, wouldn't give Florence a chance to prove herself. Instead, they gave Florence a choice: cut your nails or sit out the 4x100 relay race. No! She refused to cut her nails. Eventually, Florence cooled off. She had worked hard to come so far. Reluctantly, she gave in. She would cut her nails. But this time Florence was too late. The officials refused to let her run in the relay. Florence was disappointed, but she moved on. Even though she couldn't run in the relay, she could still compete in the 200-meter dash.

Florence put everything behind her and focused. She crouched down into her starting position, ready to run the 200-meter race. The starter shot the pistol. Off she went! Florence dashed around the curve and flew down the straight lane. Again, she ran as hard as she could, but not with a relaxed stride. She ran jackrabbit fast and crossed the finish line at an impressive 22.02 seconds. She had won her first Olympic medal. However, Valerie Brisco-Hooks had finished a hair faster.

Florence took her place on the podium with the bronze and gold winners. She stood in a somber pose, with arms at her sides, hands cupped and lips tight. It was a bittersweet win in her hometown. Florence was proud, but she wasn't truly happy with a silver medal. She was tired of finishing

second. She wasn't mad at Valerie, but was disappointed with herself.

For the first time, Florence questioned her
dream to win a gold medal at the Olympic Games.
Was it time to seek new goals? She wondered about
her future and, for over a year after the Olympics,
stopped training hard to compete. Florence ate
poorly, didn't get enough sleep and struggled to
earn money to support herself. Her Olympic dream
slipped further away.

During this time, her mother reminded
Florence to keep God near, while her father reminded her that she could face any challenge. Slowly,
she pulled herself out of her funk. She wasn't done
with her quest for Olympic gold.

Eventually, Florence began to train with
her coach, Bob Kersee, and her close friend and

Olympic teammate Jackie Joyner-Kersee. The two were now married and welcomed Florence and a new athlete to train with them.

Jackie's brother, Al Joyner, had moved from Arkansas to Los Angeles. He had never forgotten about Florence. The two worked out together and slowly began to date—often with Florence's nieces and nephews tagging along. They liked Al and played a small part in his proposal to their aunt.

In Al, Florence found a workout partner and a caring, supportive person. "He was everything I wanted in a man," she told interviewers. On October 10, 1987, Florence and Al married, and Florence legally changed her name to Florence Delorez Griffith Joyner. Florence and Al, and Bob and Jackie, became known as the "First Family of Track and Field."

....

CHAPTER 5

Going for the Gold

Even though she had questioned herself before, Florence was determined. She did not want to be remembered as being second best, and she "made the decision to try and be the best in 1988." That meant focusing!

She prayed daily, wrote her goals on paper and even on her mirror. She ate healthy meals and went to bed early to get a good night's rest. After work, she spent hours on the track to develop her form and increase her speed. To make her hip and leg muscles stronger and to improve her start off the racing blocks, Florence lifted heavy weights. To test her improvements, she traveled to Rome to compete in the 1987 World Championships, where she ran at remarkable speeds. But Florence had a secret: she knew she could run even faster!

The "First Family of Track and Field" traveled to Indiana for the 1988 Olympic trials with high hopes. The trials went well for Florence and Jackie Joyner-Kersee, but Al came in fifth for the triple jump and didn't make the men's team. Florence consoled her husband, but Al encouraged her to stay focused on her goals.

Florence made a big decision. A hard decision. She named her husband as her new coach. For Florence, her decision made sense. Her days and nights were already spent working out in the weight room with Al, training at the track with Al and racing with Al—and winning! She was grateful for her ten years with Bob Kersee as her coach, but said, "It was the perfect time for me to make that decision."

Many had counted Florence out. They only saw her unique outfits, her glamorous makeup, hair and decorated nails. Florence didn't let that bother her. She wore her outfits with pride. These included a hooded bodysuit, shimmering, fluorescent one-legged bodysuits and an all-white lace bodysuit. Her nails were shorter and colorfully painted and decorated. And she also wore a plain T-shirt with her photograph on the front, which read GOING 4 THE GOLD IN 88.

Florence was ready to prove the doubters

wrong. She ran the 100-meter dash in 10.60 seconds and broke the world record. The wind helped to push her forward, so her record didn't count. That didn't bother Florence; it only proved what she already knew: she could run even faster.

Later, dressed in a purple one-legged unitard with turquoise briefs, Florence ran the 100-meter race again and shattered the world record at a spectacular 10.49! The doubters believed her record didn't count this time either, and said, again, that she was "wind-aided." The officials checked the wind gauges and found there was no tail wind. 10.49 made Florence Griffith Joyner the fastest woman in the world!

Florence didn't just make the Olympic team. She was an Olympic sensation who gained a new nickname: "Flo-Jo." That September, Flo-Jo traveled to Seoul, South Korea, determined to win gold at the 1988 Olympic Games.

Florence surprised everyone. She not only won her two preliminary 100-meter heats, or races, she broke Olympic records each time. She moved on to the semifinals, one step before the gold-medal race! Excited, she left the starting blocks fractions of a second early. This meant she and all the runners had to return and restart the race. She overcame her "false start" and qualified for the 100-meter race. At the finals, Florence placed her feet against the blocks and let the calm surround her. She was relaxed. Ready. She heard the start and took off, using her strength, her improved form and her relaxed stride to pass everyone. Halfway into the race, her face lit up with a radiant smile, her hair flowing, Florence knew she would cross the finish line alone.

At last, Florence won a gold medal!

Four days later, Florence was more than ready for the 200-meter finals. Earlier that day, she had broken the record twice in qualifying races. The starter pistol sounded. All eyes were on Florence, and rightfully so. Her legs fully extended and she found her relaxed stride. Her body sailed almost effortlessly. Her radiant smile lit her face as she pulled away from the pack and crossed the finish line, her arms raised in victory. Overcome by her win, Florence dropped to the asphalt track, in a moment of joy mixed with tears and humility.

Florence won a second gold medal.

But how did Florence improve since the last Olympics? Murmurs and whispers spread rapidly. Many believed Florence cheated by using illegal drugs to make her stronger, increase her stamina and allow her to run faster.

While rumors spread, Florence held her head up high. She knew how hard she had worked and was anxious to answer her accusers on the track. She would show them. *"When anyone tells me I can't do anything, I'm just not listening anymore."*

Her sights were on the 4x100 relay—the race she wasn't allowed to run in 1984. Florence ran the third leg for Team USA. She grabbed the baton, sprinted 100 meters and passed the baton to the anchor, Evelyn Ashford, who pulled ahead into first place.

With that team victory, Florence won her third gold medal! Florence stood on the podium with her team and cried tears of joy while the National Anthem played.

Florence had just finished her race and was not expected to run in the 4x400 relay. She had not trained for the longer distance, but her team needed her. They said she was Team USA's best chance to win. So she lined up to run the anchor leg.

Team USA was behind the Russians, but when Florence grabbed the baton, she refused to let her team down. She fought hard against her own fatigue and pushed herself to catch the first-place Russians. Florence and the US relay team broke their own record and won a silver medal. This time, because she'd fought so hard, the silver medal won a place in her heart.

With a career total of three gold medals and two silver medals, Florence had surpassed her Olympic dreams and goals.

· ·

CHAPTER 6

Dreams and Beyond

Florence Griffith Joyner was now in high demand as a sports broadcaster, for celebrity appearances and to endorse products. What should have been a joyful time was overshadowed by doubt and accusations from others who claimed she took drugs to make her faster and stronger. To silence the doubters, Florence had undergone eleven drug tests in 1988, which included routine testing while at the Olympics in Seoul. All her tests came back clean for illegal drugs. Still, the rumors and accusations continued.

Florence knew she had pushed her mind and body beyond her limits during her training. No matter how fiercely she denied these rumors, no matter how many drug tests she passed, clouds of doubt hovered.

During those times, Florence prayed and found guidance in reading her Bible. She wanted to make the best decisions about her future. She had peace. She had clarity. She knew it was time to move on.

It was a surprise to the world when Florence announced her retirement from track and field in February 1989.

Florence went on to do what she said she would do: "everything." In 1990, she gave birth to her only child, Mary Ruth. She explored her creativity through painting colorful canvas art and writing poetry and children's books she hoped to publish. She took acting lessons and appeared on the television sitcom *227* and on the soap opera *Santa Barbara*. "*I've always been shy,*" said Florence, "*But somehow, I've never had stage fright.*"

Florence's influence on fashion was everywhere! She created her own fashion line and designed new uniforms for the NBA team the Indiana Pacers.

In 1993 Florence was both surprised and honored to be considered to co-chair the President's Council on Physical Fitness. Shortly after she was named as a co-chair, Florence was invited to join President Bill Clinton on a four-mile jog along the Potomac River to the Capitol

Building in Washington, DC. Florence was nervous! Should she slow down? She didn't want to embarrass the president. To her surprise, President Clinton ran the four miles at a brisk pace.

Florence cherished her term as co-chair and used her role to educate children about the importance of exercise, healthy eating and excelling. "I *love working with kids, talking with them and listening to them. I always encourage kids to reach beyond their dreams. Don't try to be like me. Be better than me.*"

The girl called Dee Dee reached her dreams and beyond. She was a worldwide sensation who always returned to Watts to inspire children. She began the Florence Griffith Joyner Youth Foundation and devoted her life to God, family, community and charity.

In 1998, at the age of thirty-eight, Florence passed away while she slept as a result of an epileptic seizure. To this day, her world records stand.

Florence Griffith Joyner had a dream, and she pushed herself beyond limits. She persisted in doing all she could to achieve her dreams, and—no matter what your dream is—you should too.

HOW YOU CAN PERSIST

by Rita Williams-Garcia

Florence Griffith Joyner lived a life of excellence and self-expression. Here are a few ideas to encourage your own self-expression and your personal quest to excel:

1. Make healthy choices. Include fresh fruits, vegetables and water in your daily diet.

2. Engage in some fun physical activity

for at least fifteen minutes or more each day.

3. Express yourself inside a private journal with thoughts, poems, songs and/or drawings. Decorate the cover to reflect your style.

4. Live in the plan of your dreams. Write your goals and post them where you can see them. As time goes by, change them!

5. Encourage someone else's difference and creativity.

6. Push yourself to try something new!

7. Florence Griffith Joyner experimented by making her own accessories and nail polish. Experiment! Make your own creations!

8. Spend a few minutes in quiet reflection.

ACKNOWLEDGMENTS

....

My heartfelt thanks to my longtime and dear friend Sharyn November, who put me on the right track with six little words! That was all it took, but it was what I needed.

∽ References ∾

Aaseng, Nathan. *Florence Griffith Joyner: Dazzling Olympian*. Minneapolis: Lerner Publications Company, 1989.

Arkatov, Janice. "Flo Jo Hopes the Training Pays Off for Her Role on 'Santa Barbara.'" *Los Angeles Times*, August 8, 1992. https://www.latimes.com/archives/la-xpm-1992-08-08-ca-4411-story.html.

Carlos, Marjon. "The Fastest Woman in the World Was the Most Fashionable, Too: Flo-Jo's Olympics Style." *Vogue*, August 8, 2016. https://www.vogue.com/article

/florence-griffith-joyner-flo-jo-olympics-track-and-field
-athleisure.

Cart, Julie. "Florence Griffith Joyner Has Grown Up:
Runner Who Was Always Laughed At Is Having the
Last Laugh." *Los Angeles Times*, September 15, 1988.
https://www.latimes.com/archives/la-xpm-1988-09-15
-sp-2954-story.html.

Cart, Julie. "From the Archives: She overcame an insecure
childhood to become an Olympic champion and world-
record holder." *Los Angeles Times*, September 22, 1998.
https://www.latimes.com/la-me-florence-griffith-joyner
-flojo-19980922-story.html.

Childs, Joy. "The mother behind the Olympian reveals
the spirit that was Flo Jo." *LA Watts Times*,
August 9, 2012. https://lawattstimes.com/index.
php?option=com_content&view=article&id=342:the
-mother-behind-the-olympian-reveals-the-spirit-that-was
-flo-jo&catid=12&Itemid=110.

Civil Rights Digital Library. Digital Library of Georgia.
http://crdl.usg.edu/events/watts_riots.

Clinton, Chelsea, and Alexandra Boiger. *She Persisted:
13 American Women Who Changed the World.* New
York: Philomel Books, 2017.

"Evelyn Ashford – Women's 100m – 1984 Olympic
Games," uploaded by Jim Muchmore, video, 10:36,
October. 11, 2018. https://www.youtube.com
/watch?v=soSu3fS0OB8.

"Flo-Jo in the Netherlands (2016) [English CC available]],"
uploaded by Streetwisedevil, video, 31:45, July19, 2016.
https://www.youtube.com/watch?v=W8Ewoj_Pps4.

"Florence Griffith-Joyner." CNN. https://edition.cnn.
com/2008/SPORT/04/30/florencegriffithjoyner
/index.html.

"Florence Griffith-Joyner," uploaded by Nilsondm, video,
18:59, June 5, 2012. https://www.youtube.com
/watch?v=ygV6P8UJE9w.

"Hare and Rabbit." Britannica Kids. https://
kids.britannica.com/students/article
/hare-and-rabbit/276627.

Harvey, Randy. "The Seoul Games/Day 13: Unfounded Rumors: Brazil's Cruz Implies Drug Use by U.S. Women, Then Tries to Take It Back." *Los Angeles Times*, September 29, 1988. https://www.latimes.com /archives/la-xpm-1988-09-29-sp-6085-story.html.

Hersh, Phil. "Kersee Still Waiting for Reason Griffith Joyner Dropped Him As." *Chicago Tribune*, August 7, 1988. https://www.chicagotribune.com/news/ct-xpm -1988-08-07-8801210104-story.html.

Hill, DaMaris, B. "Only Boys Have Fans: Growing Up Racing Like Flo-Jo." ABC News, February 19, 2016. https://abcnews.go.com/Sports /boys-fans-growing-racing-flo-jo/story?id=37062250.

Koral, April. *Florence Griffith Joyner: Track and Field Star.* New York: Franklin Watts, 1992.

Litsky, Frank. "Flo-Jo's Form Overtakes Her Fashion." *New York Times*, July 16, 1988. http://archive.nytimes .com/www.nytimes.com/packages/html/sports/year _in_sports/07.16.html.

"Mojave Desert." Britannica Kids. https://kids.britannica
.com/students/article/Mojave-Desert/330322.

Rose, Charlie. "A conversation with five-time Olympic
medalist, Florence Griffith Joyner," video, 13:16,
October 25, 1995. https://charlierose.com/videos/6819.

Schwartz, Kris. "FloJo Made Speed Fashionable." ESPN.
com. http://www.espn.com/classic/biography/s
/Griffith_Joyner_Florence.html.

Simmons, Ann M. "For Sun Village and Littlerock,
historic distrust persists." *Los Angeles Times*,
September 23, 2012. https://www.latimes.com/local
/la-xpm-2012-sep-23-la-me-sun-village-20120924-story
.html.

Smith, Jessie Carney, ed. *Notable Black American
Women, Book II*. Detroit: Gale/Cengage Learning,
1995. Pages 363–364.

"Sprinter FloJo Jesse Owens Winner." *Los Angeles Times*,
February 21, 1989. www.latimes.com/archives/la-xpm
-1989-02-21-sp-309-story.html.

"UCLA's Title IX 40: Florence Griffith-Joyner, Liz Masakayan." UCLABruins.com, August 14, 2012. https://uclabruins.com/sports/2012/8/14/207899352 .aspx.

"What Is the NCAA?" NCAA.org. http://www.ncaa .org/about/resources/media-center/ncaa-101/what-ncaa.

Williams, Lena. "On the Run with Florence Griffith Joyner: Still Racing Around, But for the Long Haul." *New York Times*, July 21, 1993. https://www.nytimes .com/1993/07/21/garden/run-with-florence-griffith -joyner-still-racing-around-but-for-long-haul.html.

RITA WILLIAMS-GARCIA is the celebrated author of novels for young adults and middle grade readers. Her most recent novel, *Clayton Byrd Goes Underground*, won the 2018 NAACP Image Award for Literature for Youth/Teens and was a 2017 National Book Award Finalist. Williams-Garcia is most known for her Coretta Scott King Author Award–winning Gaither Sisters trilogy that begins with *One Crazy Summer*, recipient of the Newbery Honor and the Scott O'Dell Prize for Historical Fiction. She is a three-time National Book Award Finalist. She holds a BA in liberal arts from Hofstra University and an MA in English from Queens College at CUNY. She lives in Queens with her husband.

Photo credit: Ferdinand Loyo

You can visit Rita Williams-Garcia online at
rita-williamsgarcia.squarespace.com
or follow her on Twitter
@Onecrazyrita

GILLIAN FLINT has worked as a professional illustrator since earning an animation and illustration degree in 2003. Her work has since been published in the UK, USA and Australia. In her spare time, Gillian enjoys reading, spending time with her family and puttering about in the garden on sunny days. She lives in the northwest of England.

You can visit Gillian Flint online at
gillianflint.com
or follow her on Twitter
@GillianFlint
and on Instagram
@gillianflint_illustration

CHELSEA CLINTON is the author of the #1 *New York Times* bestseller *She Persisted: 13 American Women Who Changed the World*; *She Persisted Around the World: 13 Women Who Changed History*; *She Persisted in Sports: American Olympians Who Changed the Game*; *Don't Let Them Disappear: 12 Endangered Species Across the Globe*; *It's Your World: Get Informed, Get Inspired & Get Going!*; *Start Now!: You Can Make a Difference*; with Hillary Clinton, *Grandma's Gardens* and *Gutsy Women*; and, with Devi Sridhar, *Governing Global Health: Who Runs the World and Why?* She is also the Vice Chair of the Clinton Foundation, where she works on many initiatives, including those that help empower the next generation of leaders. She lives in New York City with her husband, Marc, their children and their dog, Soren.

Courtesy of the author

You can follow Chelsea Clinton on Twitter
@ChelseaClinton
or on Facebook at
facebook.com/chelseaclinton

ALEXANDRA BOIGER has illustrated nearly twenty picture books, including the She Persisted books and *She Persisted Around the World*, both by Chelsea Clinton; the popular Tallulah series by Marilyn Singer; and the Max and Marla books, which she also wrote. Originally from Munich, Germany, she now lives outside of San Francisco, California, with her husband, Andrea, daughter, Vanessa, and two cats, Luiso and Winter.

You can visit Alexandra Boiger online at
alexandraboiger.com
on follow her on Instagram
@alexandra_boiger

Don't miss the rest of the books in the

She Persisted series!

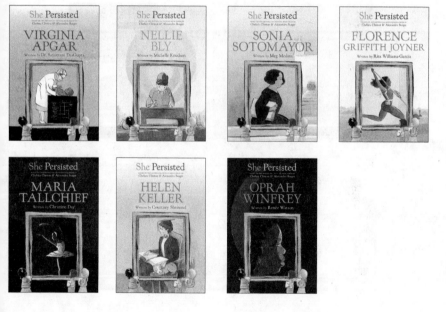